P9-DYP-378

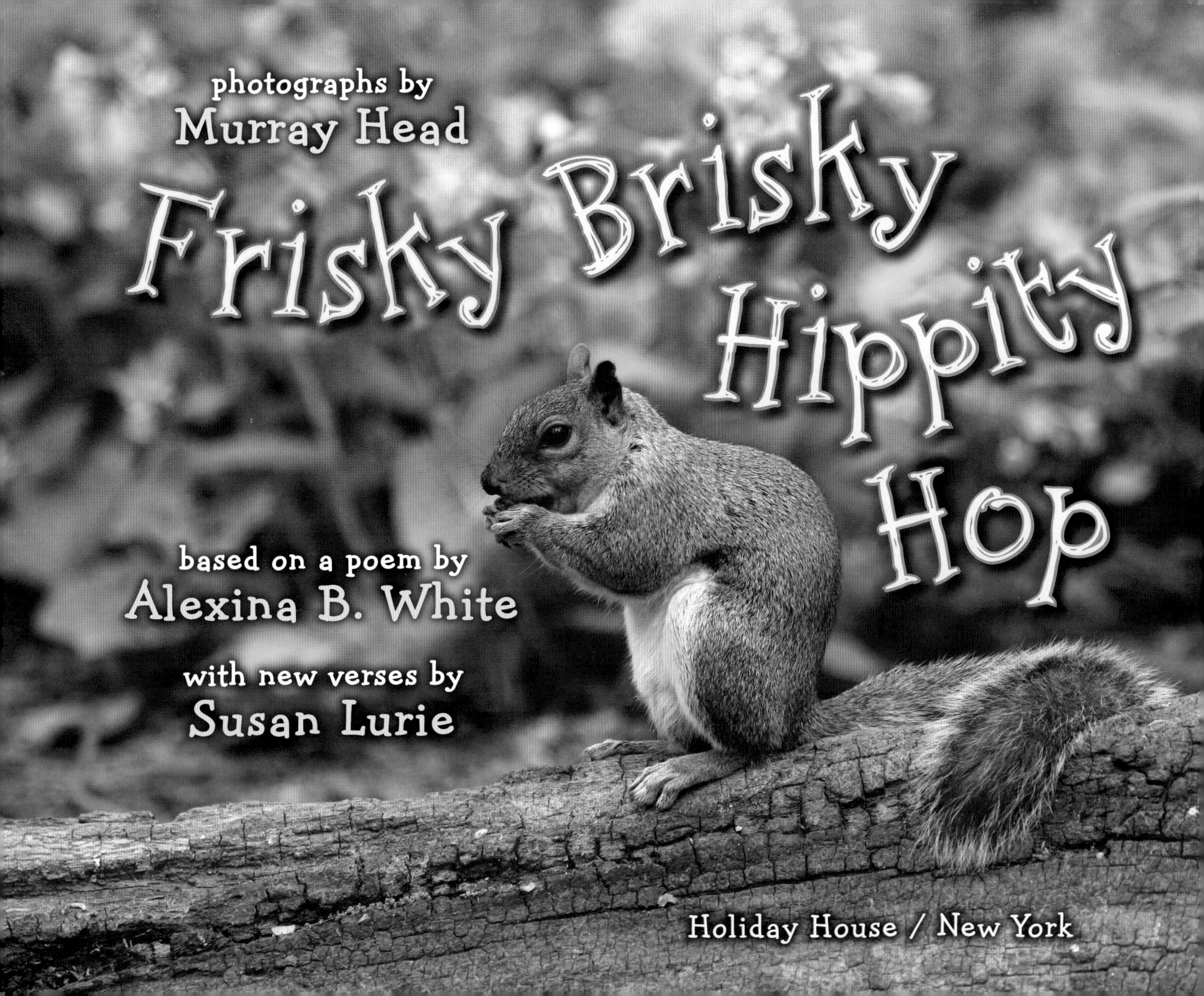

photographs by
Murray Head

Frisky Brisky Hippity Hop

based on a poem by
Alexina B. White

with new verses by
Susan Lurie

Holiday House / New York

For LV, my favorite nut!—S. L.

To the Porter family and Rosemarie—M. H.

INTRODUCTIONS

The verses in this book are a mixture of old and new. Some were adapted from a poem written more than 140 years ago by Alexina B. White. Her gleeful celebration of squirrels perfectly mirrors these present-day photos. So with just a few changes to Mrs. White's poem and some new verses written to complete the book, we have here—frisky, brisky, just for you—the enchanting story of the squirrel.

—Susan Lurie

Central Park is the jewel of New York City. Peaceful and vibrant, the park reveals the beauty of nature in all its splendor. As seasons pass, millions of visitors enjoy the constantly changing displays in ponds, fields, gardens, and woodland areas. The most popular residents of the park are the squirrels. People love to watch them, photograph them, and toss nuts to them. Squirrels are busy, scampering creatures. But for those who choose to look through the blur of their activity, a fascinating life of work and play is revealed. This book celebrates that life and provides insights into it. So come with me into the world of the squirrel—a wonderful place that delights the child in all of us.

—Murray Head

HOLIDAY HOUSE is registered in the U.S. Patent and Trademark Office.
Printed and Bound in November 2011 at Tien Wah Press, Johor Bahru, Johor, Malaysia.
The text typeface is Hank.
www.holidayhouse.com
First Edition
1 3 5 7 9 10 8 6 4 2

Library of Congress Cataloging-in-Publication Data
Lurie, Susan.
Frisky brisky hippity hop / photographs by Murray Head ; poem by Alexina B. White ; with new verses [and adapted] by Susan Lurie. — 1st ed.
p. cm.
Original version appeared as "Whisky frisky" in the book, "Little folk songs," published: New York : Hurd and Houghton, 1871.
Summary: Photographs and rhyming text follow lively squirrels through the trees and across the ground.
ISBN 978-0-8234-2410-8 (hardcover)
[1. Stories in rhyme. 2. Squirrels—Fiction.] I. Head, Murray, 1939- ill. II. White, Alexina B. (Alexina Black). Little folk songs. III. Title.
PZ8.3.L977Fri 2012
[E]—dc23
2011018742

Frisky brisky

Hippity hop

Up he goes

To the
treetop

Whirly twirly
Round and round

Down he
scampers

To the ground

Furly curly
What a tail

Tall as a feather

Broad as a sail

Giggly wriggly

Let's have fun

Leap and soar
From shade to sun

Hawk a-hunting

Can't catch me

Snickery trickery
Behind the tree!

Hide and peek

What do you see?
Slyly wily

One

Two

Three

Snapity crackity
What a treat

Break the shell
Ready to eat

Scrambly brambly
No time to rest

Making a home
In a leafy nest

Huddly cuddly

Snuggle
in tight

See you tomorrow

Good night

Good night!